Oxford International English

Student Activity Book

Liz Miles

1

OXFORD
UNIVERSITY PRESS

OXFORD
UNIVERSITY PRESS

Great Clarendon Street, Oxford, OX2 6DP, United Kingdom

Oxford University Press is a department of the University of Oxford.

It furthers the University's objective of excellence in research, scholarship, and education by publishing worldwide. Oxford is a registered trade mark of Oxford University Press in the UK and in certain other countries

British Library Cataloguing in Publication Data
Data available

978-0-19-839216-3

19

MIX
Paper from
responsible sources
FSC® C007785

Paper used in the production of this book is a natural, recyclable product made from wood grown in sustainable forests. The manufacturing process conforms to the environmental regulations of the country of origin.

Printed in Great Britain by Bell and Bain Ltd, Glasgow

Acknowledgements
Cover illustration by Patricia Castelao

Illustrations are by: Micha Archer; Patricia Castelao; Alexandra Colombo; Thomas Docherty; Jennifer Emery; Tamara Joubert; Zack Mcloughlin; Patricia Moffett; John Abbot Nez; Andrew Painter; Marcin Piwowarski; Luciana Navarro Powell; Francois Ruyer; Jan Smith; Meilo So; Nick Ward

The publishers would like to thank the following for permissions to use their photographs:

p6: Artem Loskutnikov/Shutterstock; Zlatko Guzmic/Shutterstock; p11: Aleksandra Novakovic/Shutterstock; p12: alicedaniel/Shutterstock; p16: imagebroker/Alamy; Ken Hurst/Shutterstock; xelEmbargo/iStockphoto; p20: laschi/Shutterstock; p21: Shutterstock; p22: Andrea Slatter/Shutterstock; p26: pockygallery/Shutterstock; Tribalium/Shutterstock; NEGOVURA/Shutterstock; Arcady/Shutterstock; p27: Dougal Waters/The Image Bank/Getty; p34: Peshkova/Shutterstock; p48: Willyam Bradberry /Shutterstock; Doremi/Shutterstock; hehehe/Shutterstock; Ann Precious/Shutterstock; p49: Krzysztof Odziomek/Shutterstock; gagolina/Shutterstock; Viktorya170377/Shutterstock; p50: Richard l'Anson/Getty; p55: PhotosIndia.com LLC/Alamy; p56: Richard l'Anson/Getty; Christos Georghiou/Shutterstock; Lorelyn Medina/Shutterstock; Dovgaliuk Igor/Shutterstock; ladynoi/Shutterstock; p57: Arnold Media/Getty; p78: bennyb/iStockphoto; Elnur/Shutterstock; Virinaflora/Shutterstock; M.Stasy/Shutterstock; p80: bonchan/Shutterstock; p82: Aleksandr Bryliaev/Shutterstock.

Although we have made every effort to trace and contact all copyright holders before publication this has not been possible in all cases. If notified, the publisher will rectify any errors or omissions at the earliest opportunity.

Links to third party websites are provided by Oxford in good faith and for information only. Oxford disclaims any responsibility for the materials contained in any third party website referenced in this work.

Welcome to Activity Book 1. We'll help you along the way.

Contents

Unit contents

Unit	Theme	Reading and comprehension	Writing
1	A new school	**Fiction** Narrative with a familiar setting *The Name Jar*	Fiction Writing characters' speech bubbles
2	Show me, tell me	**Non-fiction** Instructions *Signs and Labels, Our Senses, How to Make a Spinning Picture Trick*	Non-fiction Writing instructions
3	Everyday poems	**Poems** *Diggedy-do, Wobbly Tooth, Today I'm a drummer, Poppadoms*	Poetry Writing rhyming words
4	Traditional stories	**Fiction** Traditional narratives *The Magic Paintbrush, The Pumpkin in the Jar*	Fiction Writing traditional story language
5	Water world	**Non-fiction** Reports and dictionaries *Ocean Sharks, A–Z of the Sea, Sea Transport*	Non-fiction Writing questions
6	Creatures big and small	**Poems** Simple rhymes and poems *Puff!, Late One Night in Kalamazoo, A Hatchling's Song, A B, Tiny Diny*	Poetry Writing rhyming words
7	Fantasy story	**Fiction** Fantasy narrative *Ruby Nettleship and the Ice Lolly Adventure*	Fiction Writing story captions
8	About my life	**Non-fiction** Information texts and recounts *My First Year in Vietnam was Weird, Our Class Trip to the Animal Park, Alex Brychta – a Biography*	Non-fiction Writing a recount
9	Family fun	**Poem** Narrative poem *Off We Go to Mexico!*	Poetry Writing a narrative poem

Language, grammar, spelling, vocabulary, phonics, punctuation	Speaking and listening
• Initial letter sounds • Blend sounds • Sentence punctuation: full stops and capital letters • Digraph, *sh*	Questions – developing ideas and extending understanding Take turns speaking
• Labels, lists, captions • Initial letter sounds • Blend sounds • New words in context • Digraph, *ch* • Rhyming words • Instructions vocabulary	Questions – developing ideas and extending understanding Take turns speaking
• Link words to meaning • Initial letter sounds • Rhyming words • Digraph, *ch* • New words in context • Features of poetry genre	Reciting poems Expressing feelings, ideas and opinions
• Blend sounds • New words in context • Digraphs, *ch, th, sh* • Long vowel phoneme, /ee/ • Sentence punctuation: capital letters and full stops	Questions – developing ideas and extending understanding Take turns speaking Expressing ideas
• Common word endings, *–ing, –s* • Digraphs, *sh, cr* • New words in context • Common sight words, *a, and, the* • Labels • Sentence punctuation: full stops and question marks	Questions – developing ideas and extending understanding Take turns speaking Expressing ideas
• Blend sounds • Common word endings, *–ed, –ing* • New words in context • Digraph, *sh* • Rhyming words	Reciting poems
• New words in context • Digraphs, *sh, ch, th* • Blend sounds • Long vowel phonemes, /ai/ /ea/ /ee/ /ie/ /oa/ • Sentence punctuation: capital letters and full stops	Questions – developing ideas and extending understanding Take turns speaking Expressing ideas and opinions
• New words in context • Sentence punctuation: capital letters and full stops • Common sight words, *and* • Time words • Common word endings, *–s, –ing, –ed* • Blend sounds • Rhyming words	Questions – developing ideas and extending understanding Take turns speaking Expressing feelings, ideas and opinions
• New words in context • Long vowel phoneme, /ee/ • Blend sounds • Rhyming words • Verbs	Expressing opinions Take turns speaking

1 New school

A

Jamila

B

May

Johan

Kofi

Leyla

Let's Talk

Look at the children's names.
Where do you write your name?

6

The Name Jar

A **Read and respond**

1   Who is the main character in the story? Underline the name.

Mr Kim   **Unhei**   **Joey**

2   Circle all the place names where the story is set.

In a park   **On a bus**   **In a classroom**

In a zoo   **In a shop**

3 Why does Unhei blush on page 7 of the Anthology? Place a tick in the correct box.

> You blush when you feel shy or embarrassed.

She blushes because she is late for school. ☐

Unhei blushes because the children make fun of her name. ☐

She blushes because she feels sick. ☐

B Read and respond

1 How do you pronounce Unhei's name?

Yoo-hey ☐   Hey, you! ☐   Yoon-hye ☐

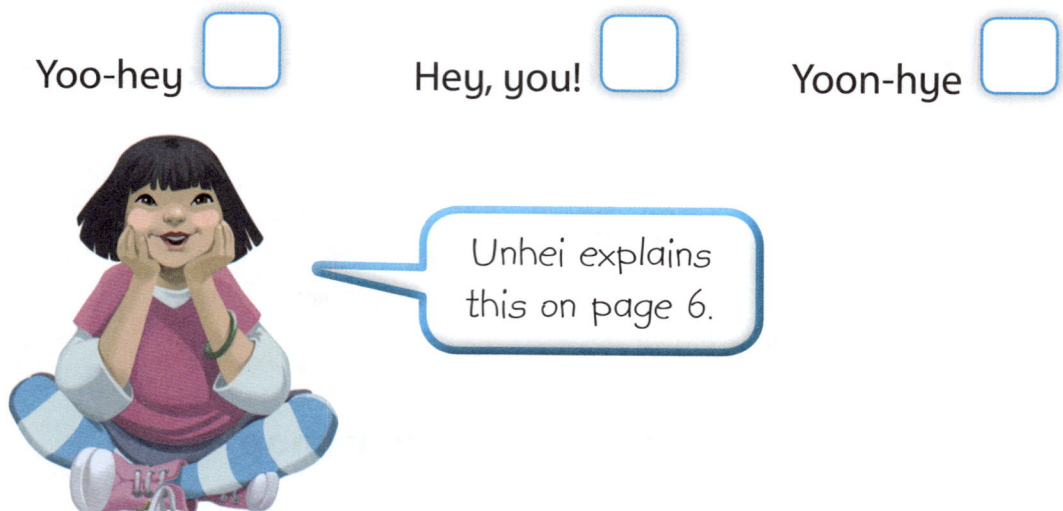

> Unhei explains this on page 6.

2 Tick the box to show if each sentence is true or false.

Unhei looks for a new name because…

	True	False
she thinks her name is too difficult to pronounce	☐	☐
her mum told her to	☐	☐
she wants to be the same as the other children	☐	☐

3 What does Unhei's name mean? Write it in the speech bubble.

Mr Kim knows! Look at page 12 in the Anthology.

_____

C What do you think?

1 Circle the ways in which Joey showed kindness and friendship to Unhei.

He held her hand.   He liked her name.

He made fun of her.   He was cheerful.

He took her into   He helped her choose
the classroom.   a name.

2 If you were Unhei, what would you have done about your name?

_____

_____

_____

Word detective

Remember that names always start with a capital letter.

A

1 **Write the missing letter to finish each name.**

J R U

_____ oey   _____ nhei

_____ alph

2 **Unjumble these names from the story and write them.**

Amanad _____   aLaur _____

Daiys _____   elaTam _____

3 **Now write your name on a piece of paper in large letters and cut out each letter. Jumble them up. Ask your partner to unjumble the letters to make your name.**

1 Sort the words that start with a **k**, **b** and **j** and write them on the jars. Two have been done for you.

jar   bus   Joey   kids   boy

bag   Korea   just   kept

k   **b**   **j**

kept   bag

2 Write some other words that start with these letters.

k_____   b_____   j_____

1 Add a full stop to this sentence and circle the two letters that should be capitals.

i don't want to be different from all the american kids

2 Circle all the words that have the **sh** sound.

> lots   shop   bus   next   brush
>
> name   jar   English

3 Now slowly read the words aloud in any order to your partner and ask them to clap each time they hear a word that has the **sh** sound.

Get writing

 **A** Draw lines to link the words to who said them.
You can find these words in the story.

"I'm Joey," said Mr Cocotos.

"How was school, Unhei?" said Joey.

"Please welcome our newest student," asked Unhei's mother.

"Helping your mother with the shopping?" asked Mr Kim.

B Fill in the speech bubbles on page 15 using the words in this cloud.

name   Unhei
My   name
want   I'm

Cross out the words when you have used them.

Show me, tell me

A

B

How to draw cartoons

Let's Talk

Where would you see signs like the ones in **A**?
Is the book in **B** a story book or a book that shows you how to draw?

16

Signs and Labels

 **Read and respond**

1 Tick the sign that tells you to do something.

2 Draw a line to match the sign with the place. One has been done for you.

classroom **door** **road**

B Read and respond

Look at the classroom picture on pages 20–21 in the Anthology to help you answer these questions.

1 Which sign tells you where you can read a book?

_____

2 Tick the signs that help you find the things you need to paint a picture.

C What do you think?

Tick the sign that helps to keep children safe.

Word detective

A Find three words that start with the same sound. Underline them.

> pen   exit   staff   paper   hands   tap   paint

B Write the missing first letter of each word, using one of the letters in the box.

> h   e   o

Wash your ____ands

Staff ____nly

Fire ____xit

Find the signs on pages 19 and 20–21 of the Anthology to help you.

Our Senses

(A) Read and respond

1 How many senses are there? Circle the correct number.

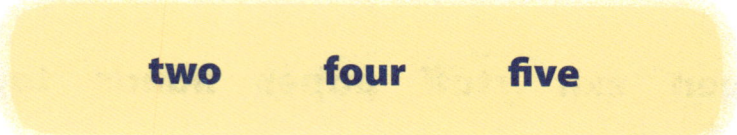

two   four   five

2 What can you do with your hands? You can tick more than one box.

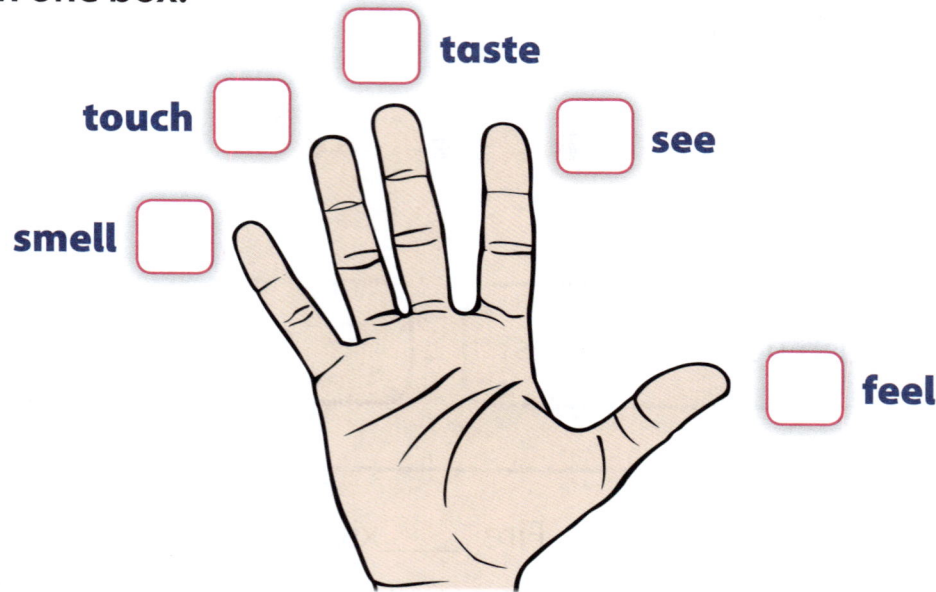

taste

touch ☐

see

smell ☐

feel

(B) Read and respond

1 Find the word 'nostrils' on page 23 of the Anthology.
Tell a friend what the nostrils do. Where are the nostrils?

_____

2   **Write one thing you can do with each sense.**

I can see _____.

I can hear _____.

I can smell _____.

I can taste _____.

I can feel _____.

C **What do you think?**

**Underline the sense which is the most important to you.
Then explain why to your partner.**

sight   **hearing**   **taste**   **smell**   **touch**

To help you, close your eyes and imagine using each of your senses.

Word detective

A On pages 22–23 in the Anthology, find a word that has the same end spelling as lun<u>ch</u>. Write it here.

_____

B Turn these jumbled letters into a word that is one of the five senses.

l   m   e   s   l

_____

C Find words that rhyme with these.

train _____ brain _____

fear _____

light _____

bee _____

How to Make a Spinning Picture Trick

A Read and respond

1 **If you do not have a hole punch, what can you use to make the holes?**

a knitting needle □   string □

scissors □

2 **What do you need glue for?**

to stick the pictures to the card □

to stick the string to the card □

to stick the jar lid to the paper □

> Read the 'You will need' list in the Anthology as well as the instructions.

B Read and respond

1 Write 1, 2 or 3 by the steps to show the correct order.

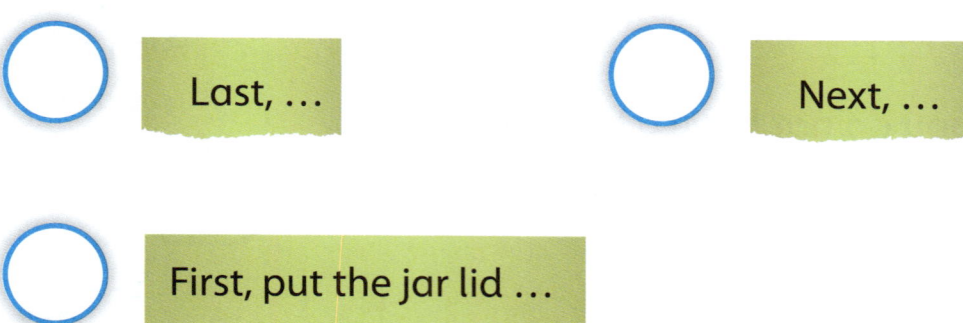

○　Last, …

○　Next, …

○　First, put the jar lid …

2 What is the trick that the toy can do?

It makes the pictures disappear. ☐

It makes two pictures look like one picture. ☐

It makes the pictures change colour. ☐

C What do you think?

Read the tip on page 26 of the Anthology. Why do you think it is better to draw in pencil first?

It is less messy. ☐   You can rub out mistakes. ☐

It is quicker. ☐

Word detective

Words like 'cut' and 'glue' tell you what to do.

A Underline the words that tell you what to do.

paper   push   put   check   lion
draw   pull   card   pencil   ask

B Look for a word in Step 8 that means 'to move fast' and write it on the line.

Get writing

 **A** Write what each sign is telling you to do, or not to do.

> Don't forget to add a full stop at the end of each sentence.

1  *Go slowly.*

2  _____

3  _____

4  _____

B Write your own sign for a door in your school.

C Draw pictures of all the things you need to make a birthday card.

Now *label* them.

27

Everyday poems

Diggedy-do

A Read and respond

What did Grandpa do?

He sneezed. ☐ He coughed. ☐ He went to bed. ☐

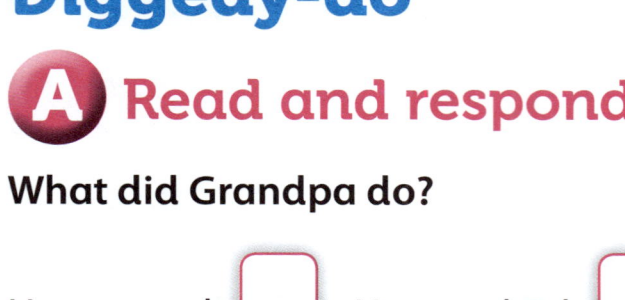

B Read and respond

What made the wheels fall off?

the speed of the train ☐   the wobbly track ☐

Grandpa's cough ☐

C What do you think?

The poem has a fast beat. Read it aloud. What do you think it is meant to sound like?

the train rushing along ☐   a clock ticking ☐

Grandpa coughing ☐

Wobbly Tooth

 **A** **Read and respond**

What is wrong with the girl's tooth?

It hurts. ☐   It is lost. ☐   It is loose. ☐

 **B** **Read and respond**

Draw a line linking each word with its meaning. One has been done for you.

tell	to feel with your hand
touch	to speak
truth	moves from side to side
bobbles	a fact or something real

Word detective

 **A** In the circles, write the number of words in the poem that begin with each of these sounds.

w ◯   b ◯

Today I'm a drummer

A Read and respond

What sort of tin does the drummer drum on?

a biscuit tin ☐

a bread tin ☐

a table-top tin ☐

B Read and respond

Where will the drummer drum at the end of the day?

on the table ☐   on the biscuit tin ☐   in bed ☐

C What do you think?

**Think of other places in the house where you could drum.
Write them below.**

I'm drumming on the _____

I'm drumming on the _____

I'm drumming on the _____

Word detective

A Write the word that rhymes with 'bread'.

_____

> Words that rhyme sound
> the same, like 'fun' and 'run'.

B Which word is repeated the most? In the chart,
write the number of times you find each word
in the poem.

> When you repeat something, you
> say or do it again and again.

drum	drumming	on	the

Poppadoms

A Read and respond

Which set of words is about eating a poppadom?

chicken and rice ☐   me and you ☐

crunch and chew ☐

B Read and respond

With a partner, clap the beat of the poem as you read it aloud. Talk about what makes it a good poem.

Word detective 🔍

A Underline the two words that have the **ch** sound as in 'chicken'.

chew

poppadoms

crunch

Get writing

Choose the correct rhyming word to complete the poem.

you   fish   hot   toast   nice

What's in the pot?
It's for dinner and it's _____ .

Is it steamy white rice?
It's something very _____ .

Is it chilli or stew?
It's something just for _____ .

Is it chicken roast?
No, and it's not beans on _____ .

Is it my favourite dish?
Yes, it's curry with _____ !

What is your favourite dish?

_____

4 Traditional stories

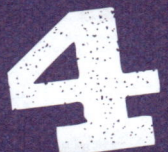

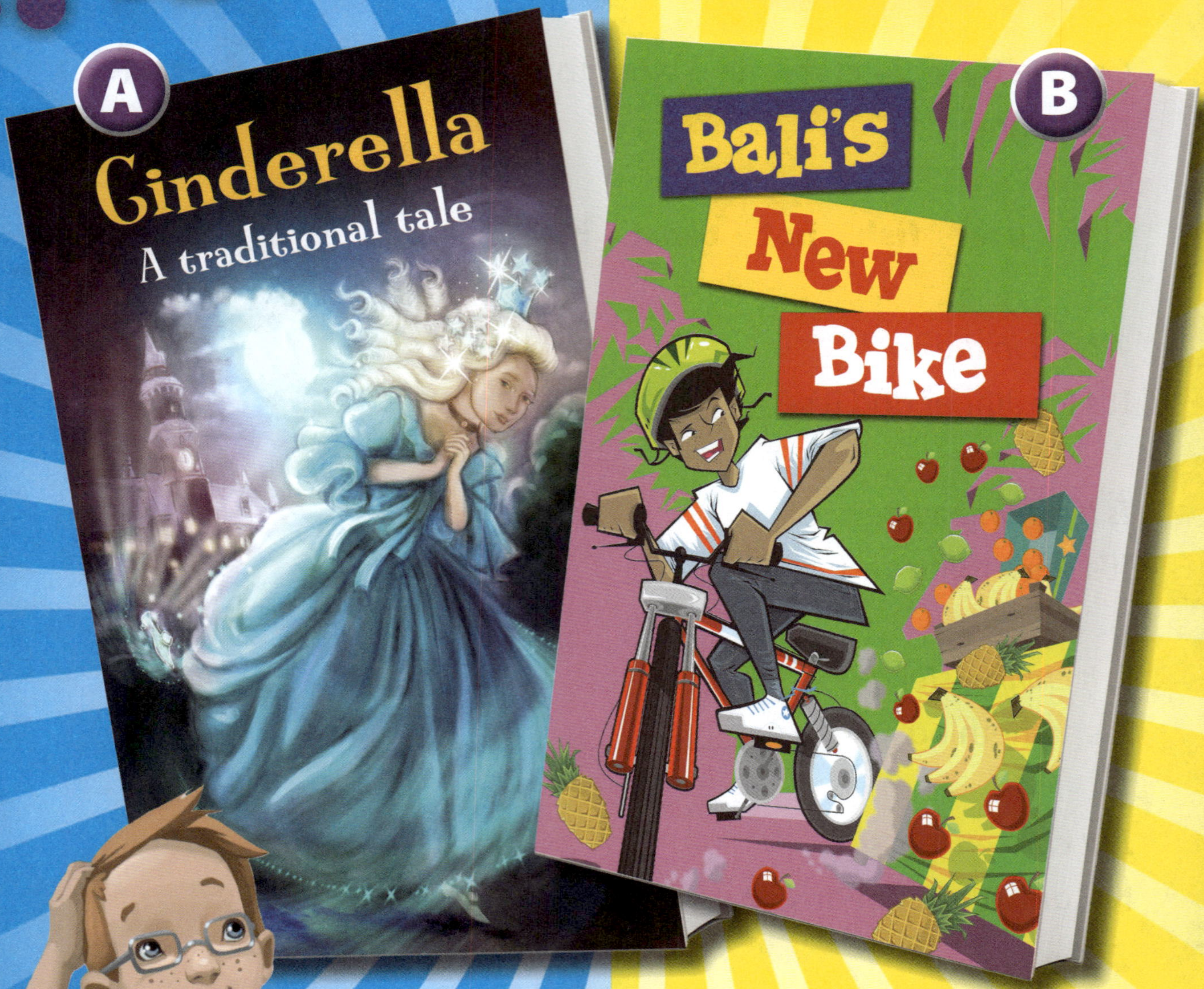
A
Cinderella
A traditional tale
B
Bali's
New
Bike

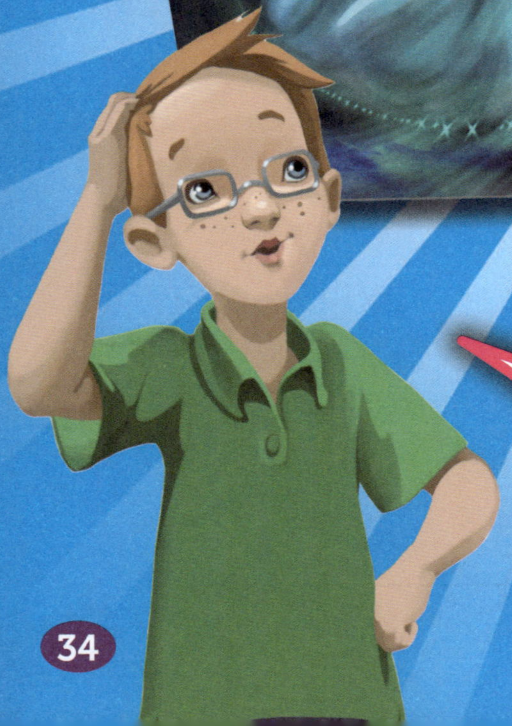

Let's Talk

What are the differences between book **A** and book **B**?

The Magic Paintbrush

A **Read and respond**

1 Stories have a **beginning**, **middle** and **end**. What happens at the beginning, middle and end of this story? Draw a line from the label to the correct picture.

beginning

middle

end

2 How does the author want you to feel at the end of the story? Tick the face that matches.

B Read and respond

1 What country is the story set in? _____

2 Tick the things that Ho used to make paints.

sun ☐   rocks ☐

plants ☐   fish ☐

gold ☐   mud ☐

3 Why did Ho paint a storm?

_____

_____

C What do you think?

A moral is a lesson the reader can learn from a traditional tale or a story.

1 **What is the moral in this story?**

Children like painting. ☐   All farmers are mean. ☐

Greed is a bad thing. ☐

2 **If you had a magic paintbrush, what would you paint? Finish the sentence, then draw it on another piece of paper.**

I would paint a _____.

What would happen if it became real? Explain here or tell a partner.

_____

_____

Word detective

Two letters together can make one sound, such as **ch** in ri**ch**, **th** in wi**th** and **sh** in paintbru**sh**.

A Find **ch**, **th** or **sh** in these words. Draw a line under the two letters. The first one has been done for you.

brush   China   cloth   fish

children   flash   ship   thin

B Write the words with **ch**, **th** and **sh** from the box below in the chart on the next page. The first one has been done for you.

| richest | shout | chicken |
| whoosh | thank | thinner |

ch words	th words	sh words
richest		

C Look for words in the story that start with **sh** as in **sh**ip. Then find words that start with **ch** as in **ch**ick. Write them in the clouds.

sh

ch

The Pumpkin in the Jar

A Read and respond

1 **What was the King hunting for?**
Tick the correct box.

fish ☐   deer ☐   pumpkins ☐

2 **What happened to the cup after the King drank from it?**

The King took it. ☐

It smashed into hundreds of pieces. ☐

It was lost. ☐

3 **Find these words in the story: curtsied   bowed**

In the story, who bowed? _____

In the story, who curtsied? _____

Tell a friend what **curtsied** and **bowed** mean.

B Read and respond

Why did the maiden say to the servant that the task would take a few months? Tick the correct answer.

The maiden had to look after her garden. ☐

The maiden wanted to make the King wait. ☐

The pumpkin would take months to grow. ☐

C What do you think?

Which story did you like best, and why: _The Magic Paintbrush_ or _The Pumpkin in the Jar_? Finish this sentence and underline your reasons. Add more reasons if you can.

I liked _____ best
because it was exciting / funny / interesting / sad.

Think about the characters and what happens in each story.

Word detective

A

1 Which words describe the maiden in *The Pumpkin in the Jar*? Draw a circle around the words you choose.

big   beautiful   silly   bad   kind   mean   clever

2 Which words describe the jar? Write them in the jar.

tiny top   chipped   thin neck
old   large   cracked

B Find five words with the /ee/ sound, as in thr**ee**, and write them here. Then add one of your own.

You can find *ee* words on Anthology pages 44, 46 and 47.

_____ _____

_____ _____

_____ _____

C Find a phrase (a group of words) that shows you that the story is a traditional tale from the past. Write it here.

_____

Get writing

 **A** Write a caption for each picture about Ho from *The Magic Paintbrush*.

_____

_____

_____

_____

_____

_____

_____

_____

 **B** Write these sentences, adding the missing full stop and capital letters.

many years ago a king lived in the forest. he was very lonely

_____

_____

 **C** Finish these sentences about *The Pumpkin in the Jar*.

Don't forget the full stops.

A k_____ met a maiden

He drank from her c_____

The m_____ smashed the cup

45

Get writing

Write a story blurb

A **blurb** is on the back of a book. It tells the reader what the book is about.

This blurb is for *The Magic Paintbrush*. Fill in the missing words with words from the box.

paints	Ho	China	tale

The Magic Paintbrush is a traditional _____ set

in _____ . An old man gives _____ a

gift. It is a magic paintbrush! Ho _____ lots of

things and they become real!

Write traditional story language

Read the sentences. Then choose the best phrase from the box to write in each gap in the sentences.

> **Every day at sunrise**   **all day long**
>
> **Long, long ago**

_____ , in a faraway wood, there lived

a poor wood-cutter. _____ , he

set off to chop wood and collect berries. He worked hard

_____ in the hot sun.

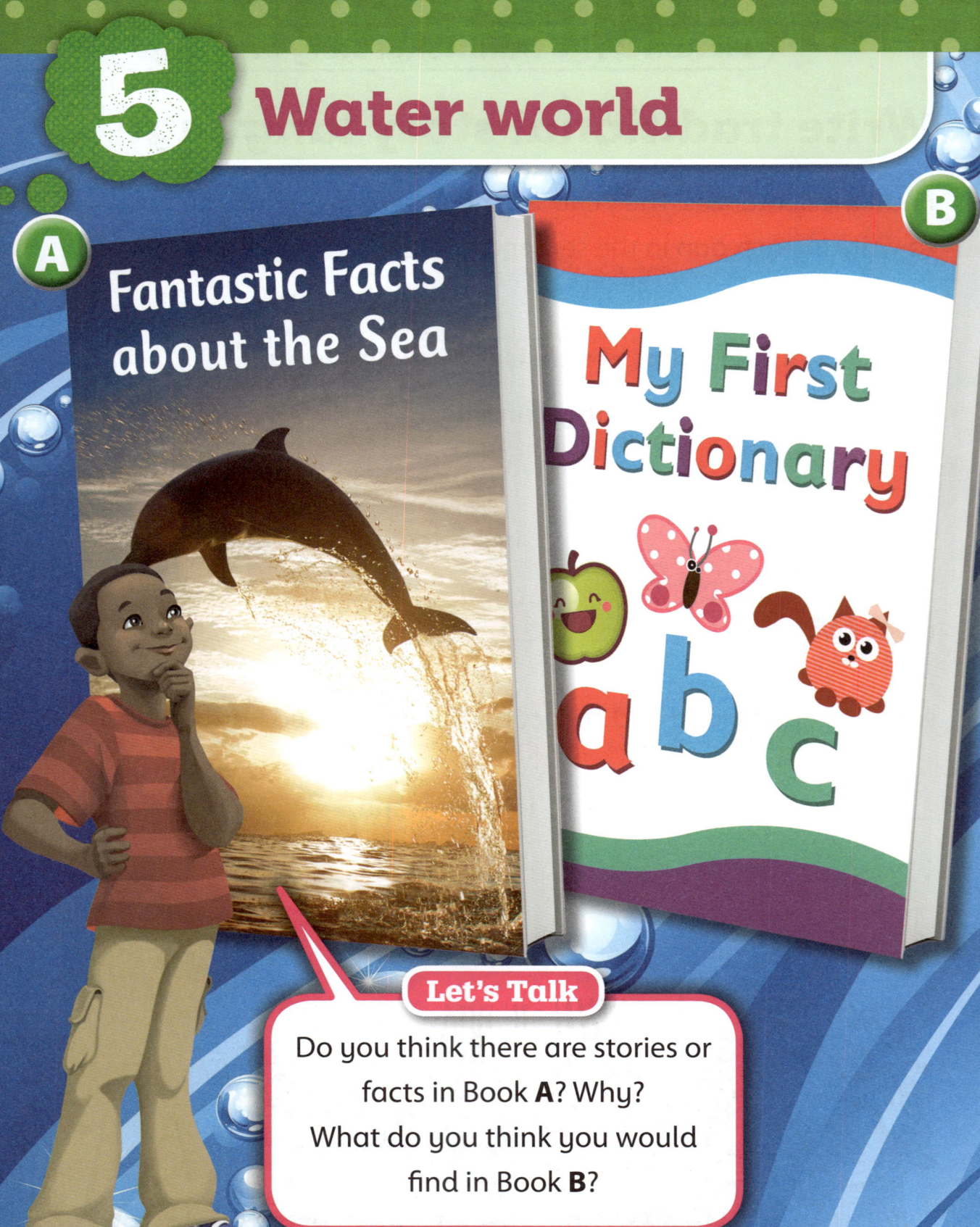

A Fantastic Facts about the Sea

B My First Dictionary
a b c

Let's Talk

Do you think there are stories or facts in Book **A**? Why?
What do you think you would find in Book **B**?

Ocean Sharks

A **Read and respond**

1 **What is a shark? Tick the correct answer.**

an insect ☐   a reptile ☐   a fish ☐

2 **Draw lines to link the words with the parts of a shark.**

snout   eye

teeth

gills

The picture on page 49 of the Anthology will help you.

3 **What do sharks use to breathe?** _____

B Read and respond

Answer these questions.

> Look at Anthology pages 50–51 to help you.

1 Circle true or false for each sentence.

Some sharks have hundreds of teeth.   **True False**

Sharks have tails.   **True False**

There are only three types of sharks. **True False**

2 Draw a line to link the shark to the words that describe it.

whale shark   dangerous

dwarf lantern shark   safe and big

great white shark   smallest

C What do you think?

Are you afraid of all sharks?

Yes ☐   No ☐

Why? _____

_____

Word detective

A **Fill the gaps with –ing or –s endings.**

A shark has a tail and fin_____ for swimm_____ . The tail

beat_____ the sea to push it along. The tail and fin_____

help steer it and stop it from roll_____ over.

B **Find as many words as you can on pages 48–51 of the Anthology that have the sh sound. Write them on the shark.**

sh can be found at the beginning or end of a word, like **sh**ark and ru**sh**.

A–Z of the Sea

A Read and respond

1 Draw lines to link the pictures with their labels.

dugong   **albatross**   **crab**   **coral**

2 Where does an anemone live?

An anemone lives _____

_____

3 What sort of book is this information from?

a story book ☐

a dictionary ☐

a comic book ☐

A dictionary has information in A to Z order.

B Read and respond

Finish the sentence by choosing one of the endings in the box.

Seals have blubber because _____

_____.

it smells good	it keeps them cool
it helps them swim	it keeps them warm

C What do you think?

A blurb is writing on the back cover of a book and tells you about the book.

Which blurb do you think is the best for the A–Z of the Sea?
Tick the best and put a cross by the worst.

A–Z of the Sea is packed with facts, pictures and maps.

A–Z of the Sea is all about things in the sea.

A–Z of the Sea is funny and a good story.

Word detective

A Choose the missing words to fill the gap.

> **and**   **a**   **the**

crab: An animal that has _____ hard shell on its

back _____ powerful claws, which lives in

_____ sea.

B Write two words from page 54 in the Anthology that begin with **cr** on the crab.

cr words

Sea Transport

 **Read and respond**

Look at pages 56–59 in the Anthology to help you answer these questions.

1 Underline the words that are headings.

> **Paddles**   **Sailing**   **Paddling**   **Sails**
> **Ancient Egyptians**   **Wacky invention**   **Propeller**

2 Circle true or false for each sentence about sailing.

The Chinese were the first people to sail.	True	False
Sailing is not a sport.	True	False
Sailing is a popular hobby.	True	False

3 Draw lines to show which boats have sails and which don't.

The Royal Clipper

car-boat   catamaran

Sails   **No sails**

dragon boat   kayak

Ancient Egyptian boat

B Read and respond

1 When were dragon boats first made?

_____ years ago.

2 Tick the word that is another name for a car-boat.

car-float ☐

sea-car ☐

amphicar ☐

Read the label on the photo of the car-boat.

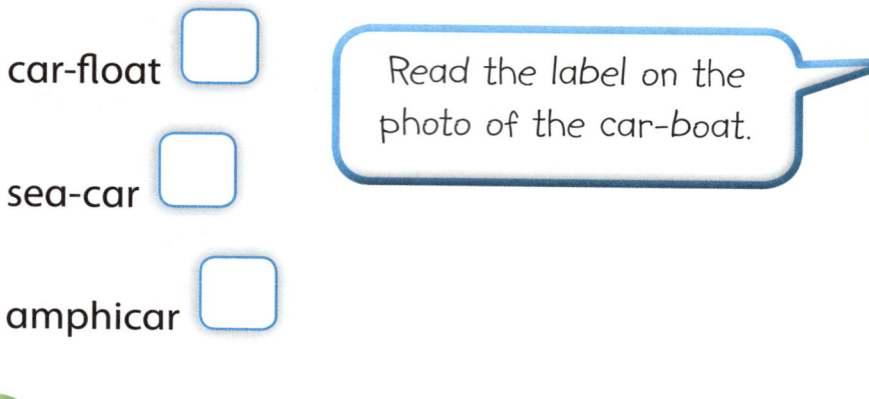

C What do you think?

Which of these things do you think are important to include in a book on sea transport? Number them 1–4 with 1 being the most important.

Submarines	Jet skis	Speed boats	Pirate ships

Word detective

A Write the correct labels for this picture.

kayak   paddle   kayaker

_____   _____

_____

B One word in each sentence needs an **–ing** ending. Circle the word.

These days, sail is a very popular sport.

Paddling is the oldest way of cross the water.

Get writing

A full stop **.** ends a sentence. A question mark **?** comes at the end of a question.

A Write the correct mark at the end of each sentence.

Is it a boat____

Yes, it's a wacky invention____

What drives the wheels____

An engine drives the wheels____

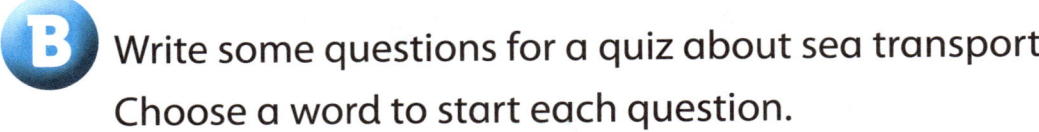

B Write some questions for a quiz about sea transport. Choose a word to start each question.

Don't forget – the question and answer should make sense together.

When   What   Who

<u>What</u> has two hulls?

Answer: A catamaran

_____ were dragon boats first made?

Answer: 2,000 years ago

_____ were the first people to use sails?

Answer: The Ancient Egyptians

_____ is at the front of a dragon boat?

Answer: A carved dragon head

Puff!

 **A Read and respond**

What hides the dragon?

one puff ☐

six puffs ☐

four puffs ☐

 **B Read and respond**

Draw lines to connect the words that rhyme.

two   four

see   you

more   me

> Read the words aloud to hear which sound the same.

 **C What do you think?**

Where do the puffs come from?

the wind ☐ the dragon's breath ☐  a fire ☐

Late One Night in Kalamazoo

 **Read and respond**

What colour was the balloon?
Write the word in the balloon, then
colour in the balloon.

 **Read and respond**

Draw lines from the animals to what they did.

camel	yodelled
poodles	danced
monkey	had a barbeque
baboons	strummed a guitar

 Word detective

 Look at the word 'Kalamazoo'. Find a small word inside
it to do with animals and write it here.

_____

A Hatchling's Song

A Read and respond

Who is speaking?

Dad ☐

Mum ☐

a hatchling ☐

Think about who 'I' is in the poem.

B Read and respond

Write numbers 1–4 in the boxes to show the order of the events in the poem.

◯ The hatchling's head is out.

◯ The hatchling pecks hard.

◯ The hatchling is free.

◯ The hatchling hurts its beak.

C What do you think?

How do you think the hatchling feels at the end of the poem?

cross and tired ☐

upset ☐

happy and tired ☐

Word detective

A Find a word with an **–ed** ending and one with an **–ing** ending on page 62 of the Anthology. Write them in the eggs.

–ed   **–ing**

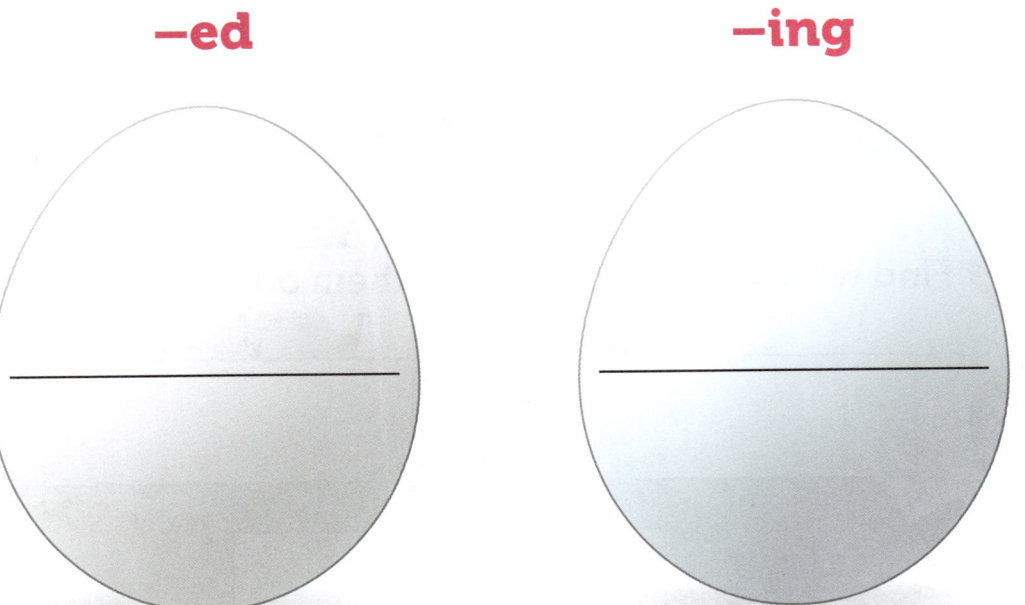

Tiny Diny

 **Read and respond**

Draw a line to link each part of the dinosaur to the word that describes it.

muscles	sharp
teeth	ripply
skin	long
tail	rough

B **Read and respond**

What word does 'Diny' mean?

_____

Word detective

A Find words with **sh** and write them on the dinosaur.

Get writing

Complete the rhyming poem using the words in the box.
Then read it aloud to a partner.

goes   tough   shoe   toes

Never fear

Here's what to do

If a tiny diny

Jumps in your _____.

Do not cry

If its skin is rough

Do not scream

If it's big and _____.

Don't forget – each
pair of words rhymes.

Pull off its socks

And tickle its _____

Quick as a flash

Away it _____!

7 Fantasy story

They set off in search of the dragon's gold

Let's Talk

Look at the pictures from the book above. Is it a real place or a fantasy land?

66

Ruby Nettleship and the Ice Lolly Adventure

A Read and respond

1 Why did the children go home?

The answer is on page 68 of the Anthology.

_____

_____

2 What happened in the story on page 71? Tick the sentences that are true.

The ice cream van sped off. ☐

The ice cream van vanished. ☐

The lolly seemed to glow. ☐

The lolly suddenly turned green. ☐

3 Find words and phrases in the story that tell you about the shoot. Write them on the shoots.

Look on pages 73 and 74 in the Anthology.

B Read and respond

1 **What grows from the shoot? Circle all the correct words.**

> a van   poles   ladders
>
> roller coaster   roundabout   swings
>
> ice creams   a shop   slides

2 **Why did the whole city stop on page 77?**
List your reasons.

> Look at the illustrations on pages 76 and 77 of the Anthology to work out why everything stopped in the city.

_____

_____

_____

3   How does Ruby feel during the adventure?
Choose a word and write it under each picture.

puzzled   bored   excited
amazed   sad   shocked

_____   _____

_____   _____

_____   _____

4 Ruby's thoughts seem to make the shoot turn into
different things. If you were Ruby, what would you wish
the shoot to change to next?

_____

_____

C What do you think?

1 Look back through the story and think about Ruby.
Circle the words you think describe her.

> shy   adventurous   quiet
>
> bossy   friendly   kind

Think about the first thing she did when the shoot playground grew over the street. She shared it with friends.

2 What do you think Ruby is thinking in this picture?
Write it in the bubble.

_____

_____

_____

_____

A fantasy story is often set in an imaginary world.

3 All of these describe the fantasy world in Ruby's adventure. Which one do you think is the best description? Tick a box or write your own description.

a fantastical playground ☐

a world where adults play ☐

a world in the sky ☐

_____

4 Which part of the story do you like best? Finish the sentence.

Best of all, I like the part when _____

_____ because

_____

_____

Word detective

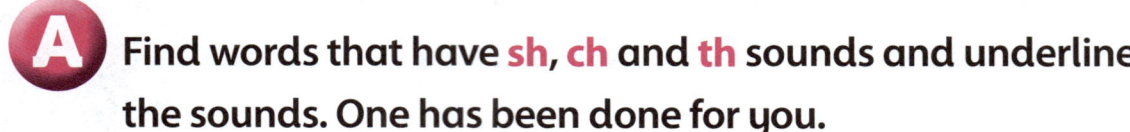

A Find words that have **sh**, **ch** and **th** sounds and underline the sounds. One has been done for you.

1 Now there was nothing to play on and the children began to wander home.

2 "Thank you," she remembered to say, but when she looked up again the ice cream van had vanished.

3 The shoot shot up into the air, nearly hitting her on the nose.

Write other words that start with these pairs of letters.

sh_____ ch_____ th_____

B Write **ai**, **ea**, **ee**, **ie** or **oa** to finish the words.

1 The lolly was gr____n.

2 When she looked up ag____n the ice cr____m van had

vanished.

3 "Wow!" cr____d Ruby.

4 They made a trolley roller c____ster!

C Circle the letters that should be capital letters and add the full stops. One has been done for you.

hello.

there are not many people here today

The swing broke

do you want a lolly?

yes, please

it's my last

Thank you. i like the green wrapper

Get writing

Part A Story captions

Finish the captions under the illustrations.

The swing broke.

A shoot and sw_____
grew.

They went to the
_____ .

The lady gave Ruby an ice
_____ .

They _____

_____ _____

supermarket.

The whole _____

ground to a halt.

Ruby p_____ the
lolly stick into the ground.

Ruby picked up her
fr_____s.

Part B

Order the events in **Part A** by numbering them 1–8. The first
one has been done for you.

A

Dear Gran

We arrived in Brazil on Monday. On Tuesday we went to the beach. Yesterday we saw parrots in the forest! Tomorrow we are camping by a river. We miss you.

Love from Nath

32A, Harbour View,

Kolkata

B

My Diary

Let's Talk

What sort of things would you write on the card in **A**?

What sort of things would you write at the end of each day in **B**?

My First Year in Vietnam was Weird

 **Read and respond**

1   Write the correct place name in the sentence.

> **Melbourne**   **Hanoi**   **London**

D'Arcy moved from _____ to Vietnam.

2   On page 78 of the Anthology, what two things does the writer say he missed? Circle the answers.

> **traffic**   **footpaths**   **traffic lights**
>
> **Tae Kwon Do**   **football**   **motorbikes**

3   What does D'Arcy do instead of playing football?

_____

4   What is Vietnamese pho?

_____

B Read and respond

Order the events in time by numbering them 1–4.

◯ Started Tae Kwon Do

◯ Missed Melbourne's traffic lights

◯ Met Jono

◯ Started school

C What do you think?

What things made the writer feel happy to be in Vietnam in the end? Write them here.

> Have you ever moved to a new place? What did you like or dislike about it?

Got a black belt in Tae Kwon Do

_____

_____

_____

Word detective

A Write the sentence, putting in capital letters and a full stop in the correct places.

> learning to speak french was hard, so i wanted to go back to the english school

_____

_____

_____

B Join the sentences by adding 'and'. Write out the new sentence below.

I can speak French. I can speak a bit of Vietnamese.

_____

_____

_____

Our Class Trip to the Animal Park

 **Read and respond**

Draw lines to match the times to the captions.

10 past 8

They got to the Animal Park.

They got back to school.

lunchtime

9 o'clock

The coach set off.

They sat by the lake.

4 o'clock

 **Read and respond**

What is the name of the Animal Park?

Remember to look for information in the pictures as well as the text.

C What do you think?

1 Did the writer enjoy the day? Circle Yes or No.

Yes   No

How do you know?

_____

_____

2 On a sheet of paper write down everything that Rosa did. With a partner, talk about whether you would like her to be your friend. Explain why.

Word detective

A Circle the words or phrases that tell you *when* something happened.

the   finally   her

went   during the afternoon   at 4 o'clock

spider   roared   at lunchtime

B Draw a line to link the labels to the correct animals at the Animal Park.

hippo

spider

giraffe

panda

lion

tiger

C Add numbers to the animals above to show the order in which they were seen by the class.

Alex Brychta – a Biography

 **Read and respond**

Tick the sentence that is true.

Alex Brychta writes stories about Biff, Chip and Kipper.

Alex Brychta draws and paints illustrations
for story books.

Alex Brychta teaches children how to paint.

 **Read and respond**

In which city was Alex born?

_____

Read the captions on
page 85 of the Anthology
to find the answer.

C What do you think?

How interesting is Alex's biography? With a partner, list one idea for extra information and one idea for an extra picture to make the biography more exciting.

I would include information on _____

_____

I would include an extra picture of _____

_____

Word detective

A Add the missing –s, –ing and –ed to this sentence.

Later, children in lot_____ of countries start_____

read_____ Rod and Alex's books!

When you have finished, read the sentence to check it sounds right.

B Draw lines to join up the two parts to make whole words.

st   art

dr   ee

tr   aw

Now write the words here.

_____ _____ _____

C Write two words from the box that rhyme with each word in the list.

broom   look   tool   cool   cook   groom

book   _____ _____

room   _____ _____

school   _____ _____

Get writing

Part A

Write numbers 1–6 to show the order in which you do these things on a school day.

◯ Start lessons

◯ Have breakfast

◯ Go home

◯ Set off to school

◯ Play with my friends

◯ Get dressed

Part B

Imagine you have been to a zoo. Fill the gaps in the sentences on the next page with words from the boxes. Some words have been started for you.

insects
lions
tigers
hippos
pandas
penguins

lunch
snack
drink

First
Next

Pick whichever animal words you like!

We got to the zoo at 10 o'clock. F_____ , we went

to see the giraffes. N_____ , we went to see the

_____. After a dr_____ and a

sn_____ we went to see the _____ .

At 1 o'clock we sat down near the lake and had

_____ .

In the afternoon, we saw spiders and _____ too.

At 4 o'clock it was time to go home.

89

Family fun

Off We Go to Mexico!

A Read and respond

1 Underline the word that tells us that more than one person went to Mexico.

We swim in turquoise water and build castles on the beach.

2 Put the events in order by adding numbers 1–4.

( ) We wave our flags   ( ) Home we go from Mexico

( ) Off we go to Mexico!   ( ) We climb amazing pyramids

3 What makes the butterflies want to fly?

_____

You can find the word on page 93 of the Anthology.

B Read and respond

1   Draw lines to show where these things were.
    The first one has been done for you.

market day	capital
festival	native villages
dancers	village square
museums	plaza

2   On the train, why did they 'dare not look below'?
    Tick the right answer.

They were afraid of falling. ☐   There was a tunnel. ☐

The market was below. ☐

C What do you think?

Read the line from the poem that you like best to your
partner. Explain why you like it.

Word detective

A Write three words from the poem that have **ee** in the middle.

> **ee words**

B Find a word in the poem for each picture and write it under the picture.

p_____

t_____

b_____

f_____

C With a partner, find the pairs of words in the poem that rhyme. Write each rhyming word next to its partner below.

Rhyming words are not always at the end of a line.

beach _____

steep _____

eat _____

bands _____

twirl _____

feet _____

way _____

zoo _____

Get writing

Part A

Look at these pictures of things to do on holiday. Tick three that you would like to include in a poem.

Climb a hill ☐

Visit a rainforest ☐

Watch whales from a boat ☐

Kayak in the sea ☐

Part B

Now write your holiday poem. Choose some verbs from the cloud and the places from the opposite page and write some lines below. The first two are examples.

feel   climb

visit   play   cook   watch

touch   hear   see   taste

kayak   walk

We climb a hill.

We hear birds in the rainforest.

We _____

We _____

We _____

We _____

What do you think?

Which story, poem or facts did you like best? Draw a picture below of something you enjoyed learning about.

Write two sentences about what you liked best and why.